PEARL
COLLECTOR

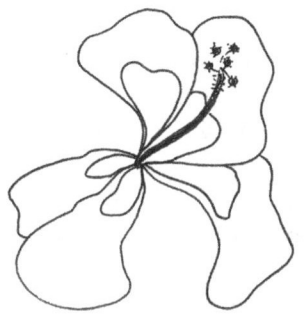

KALIE DEBELAK

Pearl Collector
Kalie Debelak

Book Design by Emily Ruf
Illustrations by Kalie Debelak
Pearl images on cover from Vecteezy.com

First U.S. Edition, 2022

Library of Congress Control Number: 2022911210

Print ISBN: 979-8-9863487-1-1
Ebook ISBN: 979-8-9863487-0-4

Published in the U.S.A. with assistance by
Spoonbridge Press, Saint Paul, Minnesota

I dedicate this work to those of us who fell in love when it was inconvenient. For those who have ever been, or are, in love with multiple people and don't know how to move forward without making an absolute mess of themselves. This is for the period of longing that makes you confront your deepest desires and for the purest pleasure that follows the fulfillment of those wishes.

This is for the hopeless romantics, the people who grew up believing in the idea of soulmates but are no longer sure now, in their adult lives, if it's true. This is to those of us who are dedicated to healing and finding beauty in the process, no matter how soul-crushing, earth-shattering, or energy-poaching. This is for you, who are brave enough to keep loving anyway.

Lastly, this is an ode to the short-lived and untested romances that remain pearls in our memories.

CONTENTS

Preface.................................... vii

Falling 1

Tension 5

Longing.................................... 9

Pleasure...................................21

Breaking 29

Healing....................................45

Reclaiming.................................65

Acceptance.................................75

Reflections 83

Author's Note 87

Gratitude 89

PREFACE

I want to be upfront about where this story comes from so there is little room for speculation. In college, I found myself in love with two people at the same time. The first was my high school boyfriend, and the other was my ex-boyfriend's embodied opposite. Where my old love was extremely ambitious and anxious, my new love was relaxed and easygoing with little worry for the future. My old love's emotions were never hidden; my new love rarely let on that anything was troubling him.

The overlap of these two relationships began my second year of college. I had been with my high school boyfriend for almost two years when I met a young man from class. It felt like love at first sight—it really did. I knew he and I had a connection that came right out of a past lifetime together. I also knew I couldn't stay with my boyfriend knowing I felt this way about someone else.

Once I ended my old relationship, I dated my new love on and off for about a year and a half. Then, the summer after my senior year of college, I decided I was done with all the wishy-washiness and declared I was going to visit him across the country to figure "us" out. We (or so I thought) decided to give our relationship a shot. After so much inner turbulence, wondering if we would ever be together, we finally were! I was ecstatic. The relationship I dreamed about was finally happening . . . and it was a shit show.

Unfortunately, while I was committed to making it work, he was not. In retrospect, I should have seen it coming. But I didn't, blinded by my idea of what we could be. Nevertheless, it is this that I consider my greatest love and heartbreak.

If you find yourself on a similar journey, you may recognize many of these experiences. Maybe you're on that journey now—know that your path may be different. Like me, you may spend more time in certain stages along the way, but the steps you take and the places you end up are all your own.

Whatever path your journey takes, I hope my words unlock something in you, whether it be the first step in grieving a loss or simply the reminder that showing up for yourself and your people is an act of bravery.

FALLING

Am I merely distracted,
or is my soul
telling me there is
something worth searching for . . .

For practicality
or for whimsy?

There were
two, and
they were
together—
finally!

Nothing in the world
more satiating
than the first
kiss we shared

—2/19/20

TENSION

There is a seed inside of me
that my lover will not water.
He doesn't even know
it's a part of my soil.
What am I to do?
I have found the others with
the same seed in their hearts—
my lover is not one of them.

(there is an emptiness between us now)

I am
trying to express a change
that cannot
be put to words.
It is sensation, and spiritual.

I am expanding.
Maybe he is, too.

If I love two,
is one truer
than the other?

I think of you
when with him,
and with you, I think
of him, less so,
but still.

LONGING

When I
imagine myself going
back to a home
I no longer wish
to inhabit,
I don't know
if I can go, knowing
I'll be breaking my own heart.

—*thoughts from study abroad*

How many selves am I?
How many do I carry
in this single body?

I feel like myself,
then me again,
but different.

I want to melt
under your hands until
time stops and God
comes to consume
us with light and fire.

The torture of lovers who must
sleep apart is that of an
asymptote. Hyperbolic,
closer and closer
but never t o u c h i n g .

You are in my
headspace, smiling,
and I love you there.
Of course, I love you
here, too.

Can we always be
this in love?

I see you every night in
a movie behind my eyelids.
I watch myself kiss
you and hold your
hand against my skin.

Are you dreaming
of me, too?

Your lips
press into my neck,
your fingers
make gentle circles . . .
the heat of your
breath fills me with
light.

I miss your sweetness
and your taste.

We let our tongues
dance while water falls
and drips down
the small of my back,
where your hands hold on,
making our skin
wet.

Oh, the pleasure of you.

No, there is nothing more.
There could have been
if you'd wanted it, too.

The hibiscus was a kiss
you handed me before
our lips could ever touch.

I held it, rolled it in my palm,
and put it in my hair.
I closed my eyes,
glad to be wearing you.

The hibiscus was something
to hold when it was
your hand I couldn't.

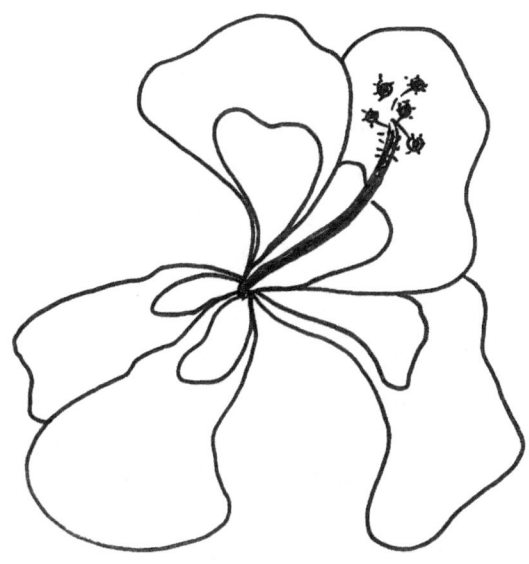

PLEASURE

I didn't think I could
come until I did, and
I felt fuller.
I was no longer restricting
myself from any possibility
of who I wanted to be in a
moment of time.

I ran into the ocean completely naked and have never felt so free.
The water needs to be everywhere, around and inside.
I belong rolling in the sand.

She waits in
the water
for the rush.
As quickly
as it arrives, it
is over.

When the energy
flows, it does
so freely.
Our bodies together,
enveloped in the blanket
of true addiction:
dopamine and desire.

I want the
sweetness of
your tongue on
me until my body
is warm with
heaven and light.

Last night we danced
in Studio One:
you walked in and
grabbed my hand,
giving it a squeeze,
smiling at me.

When we graze
I always know it's you.

BREAKING

You made a ring from the air
as we lay on the sand
on the beach of Tahoe.
You slipped that immaterial circle
onto my finger and asked me to marry you.
Of course I said yes, and I made my
own ring for you, darling. I've been
waiting a long time for this.

I put it on
your delicate finger and asked you
to marry me, too.
I wouldn't be the one to walk away
because you were every dream
of mine in flesh.

But a sudden change of heart was always
looming, and for us, it was
inevitable.

You broke those invisible
rings and cast them away as though
the words you spoke hadn't been bottled
up for years before they fell from your
strawberry lips. You broke my heart
in a way that had been
unimaginable to me because

for the first time, I decided to trust
you completely.

But words of honey are not actions of gold,
and the colors you fed me: unsustainable
and temporary.

I'd do anything to share space, food,
a bed with you again.
No matter where you were, you
always felt like home to me.

—*jaded*

You let us deteriorate,
and I had no choice but
to let it happen
because to you, it wasn't worth
a discussion. You were done,
and it had absolutely nothing
to do with me.

I wasn't even worth a
damn phone call (?!).

You sounded
too premeditated for a
"sudden change of heart,"
you coward.

Some dreams must die.
I will not betray myself
for an effortless fantasy
you only gave half of yourself to.

If you wanted me,
you would have made the effort,
released your ego
and your selfishness.

I was ready for
difficult. I wasn't
ready to be
trapped in your

i l l u s i o n .

It's not that you didn't love me,
you just didn't love me
enough (to try).

It wasn't dramatic.
You left and the door closed gently behind you.

I made myself a cup of coffee and pretended not to notice.

It didn't sound like you
saying goodbye.
That was the saddest part
of all.

My belief in you is crumpled
and torn. For my own sake
I am throwing it away.
I don't want
to be able to feel this
for you ever again.

—*goodbye & fuck you*

You told everyone I was different
yet treated me like I was ordinary,
repeating your cold and distant
patterns. Is it because I made you feel
something in your bones that you were
angry with me? Is it
because I saw you cry or asked
you to confront the shadows
you'd spent 22 years
running away from?
I loved when you cracked
down the center and opened,
baring your heart to me. I thought
you were the most beautiful
soul I'd ever met, and still
you resent me?

The way we saw each other hurt us both—
pedestals
        worship
                fiery wanting.

(I know I hurt you, too.
I am not all good.)

I wonder if we ever see the truth of people.

There is a sadness about you.
A shame you haven't held hands with.
I can see it in your eyes and in
the way you curl up on your side
at night as you fall asleep.
I can't ask you about it
now, but I'll be around
when you're ready
to talk about it.

(I still love you.)

—*observations from your intimate lover*

I am certain I'll always wish
there was more. Of you, of us,
of our time together.

We were a winning hand,
a lucky chance that
kept me
coming back.

I still meet you in my dreams.
I miss waking up next to you
with the sun in the window,
kitten on the sill,
and your head on my breast.

Our souls will find each other again (they must!),
and I will love you there/then, too.

HEALING

I loved you on
purpose. Not because
it was easy or
convenient, but
because I wanted to
choose you and
keep on choosing you.

You were never
a waste of time
to me. I always
wanted all my
seconds to be shared.
But now
I know they won't be,
so I'll be grateful for the time
we had and dive into my future.

A better place.

Something different.

How can we wait on something for so long, and once we have it, we kick and scream like it's our captor-oppressor?

I don't deserve to be an option or to beg
for scraps of your attention. I shouldn't have
to ask you to show me you love me—
ultimately, there is a difference between
someone who loves you and
someone who knows how to love you.

No matter how badly I want you to know how,
I cannot change you. I can't make you want me
or be willing to give me your time. So
I walk away.

I know how to love me.
If you won't meet me there
in that sacred place, then
I won't invite you anymore.

What-ifs are taunting me.
So I captured them in my
butterfly net and sent them
down the Mississippi in a box
I found under my bed next
to the haunted dust bunny,
a friend of my ghost.

—*the hypothetical will haunt you*

I've kept space for this
in my heart for three
years despite all
the actions screaming
that I shouldn't.
For that, dear heart,
I am sorry.

—I should have let go sooner

Things don't
feel great right
now, but perhaps
they will
feel better soon.

—*hope*

My deepest emotions are temporary
and unstable like a small pebble
on a turbulent ocean shore,
but they are completely and
divinely mine.

Pushing away
because I am scared is far more
heartbreaking than leaning in
and not having it work out.

—*learn from your mistakes*

If we know too hot
feels like too cold, and too
cold burns like fire,
why then do we neglect
the blurred line between
pain and pleasure,
love and violence?
The two are so much
the same we may never really know
which is the truth of our experience.

—*it wasn't butterflies*

You are not
worthy of the
pedestal I put you on.

The older I get, the more questions
I have about the unconditional.

Unconditional love?
You can expect love in return.
Unconditional respect? Should
you not demand respect, too?

Boundaries do not
have to be barriers, and
conditions do not have
to be ultimatums.

—*there is a balance*

I haven't dreamt of
you in weeks.
I am so much
happier this way.

—*getting rest*

I've lived more now. I've seen more, too. We both had every right to be angry and hurting.

The weather changes
inside us, too.

I keep choosing what
is best for me, even
when it's fucking hard.

—*daily affirmation*

If I do not find it
within myself,
then I will not have it.

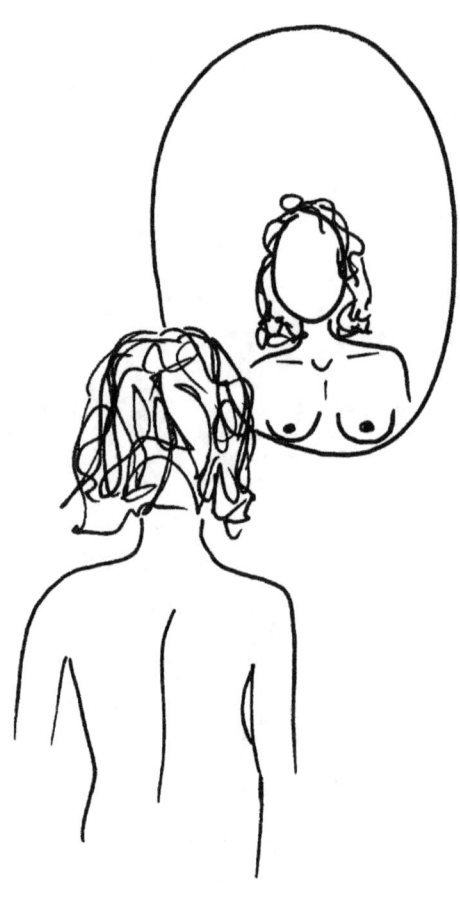

RECLAIMING

People grow and change in all relationships. There isn't a single kind of relationship that is exempt from the work of reacquainting and continuing to meet the other person in each new self.

Wanna know something wonderful? There is no "right" or "wrong" next step. The step will be. The opportunities exist. How daunting and how freeing, that you get to choose where you go next. Perhaps this is unexpected, or maybe you've been planning it for years.

Either way, your path will be beautiful, and you will find a way to thrive.

Call me a damned fool
but I have never loved
so big in my life and I'm
proud that I did it even
though it wasn't returned.
I wasted not my energy
or my time. Not even the
space in my heart or
mind, not even my pleasure.
It was a full and all-
consuming love that I gave
so freely.

For this I am one of the
bravest people I know.

I'm having the stones we found made into something beautiful for myself. They have nothing to do with you—empty words and weightless promises. They are a testament to my own intrepidness and my sweet ability to love others fiercely, and with absolutely everything I have.

Maybe it's not going to be
butterflies and sweaty palms.
Maybe it's not instant
attraction, but a gentle sharing
of interests and budding
friendship. Maybe
the sparks aren't flying
everywhere, but
you feel them in your chest
during the awkward
conversations because they matter.
Maybe it's not going to be
so abrupt, but more
like a gentle touch and
steady presence. Maybe it's
feeling safe and honest
and vulnerable in a way you haven't
known before.
Maybe it's all softer.

I can't hear what
you say to me in the
privacy of your mind.

How terrifying it is to
trust.

If you are
trusting, you are heroic
and I am proud of you.

You deserve a love that loves you on purpose.

ACCEPTANCE

Using the miles meant to see you
to see someone else.

My body hurts. It's anxiety
twisting around inside of me.
It's you moving out, becoming
untangled from my soul.
Our vibrations created
the most beautiful music I'd ever
heard, and so I guess now I will
have to trust that someone else
will make beautiful music with me, too.

You must've gotten my letter.
You're leaving me; I've already
left you and it still makes me ache.
I shake and shiver, but not because
I've met my small death with you
wrapped in my warmth.
I shake because I cry. I shiver
because I am cold. It's not the same
living without you.

It's different now.

You and I had a great love story.
I lived a fairytale, and I don't
think I'd do it again.
Because I didn't just fall in love.
I fell through your fingers and
into your bed. I fell into the
chest, sheltering your bloody heart.
I fell into the illusion and
the hope of it all. I fell into your
arms and into your lips. I opened
myself to you, falling into the
pit of your taking. Damn me, a giver.

I fell back to earth, and I saw
you stuffing my heart into your
back pocket instead of tending
to her in your hands.
Then, of course, I fell apart.
Then, again, into myself.

I will be a collector of loves.

Knowing that I am my own
greatest love story,
I will collect these pearls
and wear them as buttons
on my sweater. They will be
undone and fall off.

I'll sew them back on because
they showed me something
I can bring with me on my
way to find another delicate,
shiny, glimmer of hope
who gives no promise of the end.

And it doesn't matter, because
I found something. I get to
hold it and keep what I want of it,
letting the rest go. I get to
remember and forget. I choose
to wear you or to not wear you
and fold you up for a drawer
rarely opened.

I get to hang on only as much as I want.
I will be a collector, but never

will I keep a pearl so long that
it begins to take beauty away from me.

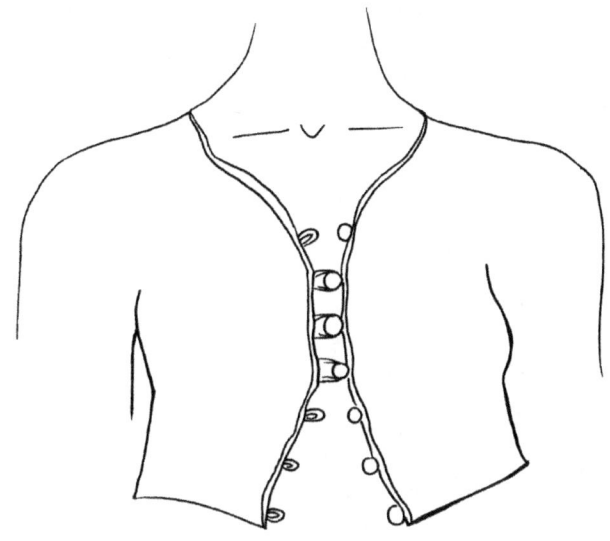

I listened to a podcast today
and it said something like
"the love story of your life
is really an autobiography."
I like that. It's me. It's always been me.

REFLECTIONS

Sometimes, I think I am two souls in one body. It feels like there are two people who want to live to their fullest potential, but I am only allowed to choose one. I can imagine myself living two very different lifestyles (perfectly represented by my two loves, old and new) and being happy and authentic with either one. This is confusing.

Through it all, I have learned that there are others who, like me, need both structure and free flow, loud and quiet, responsibility and opportunity for risk. What I felt was lacking in my old relationship, I sought out in a new one. I forgot that maybe, there is a way to have both, to hold the perceived dichotomy of two disparate people in one human.

I am that human. I am the person who needs both-ness. As emotionally exhausting as these relationships turned out to be, they taught me valuable lessons. I have learned how to discern my feelings and what I can do about them, how to be okay with doubt and distance, how to express anger, grief, and reconciliation, and, ultimately, how to find wholeness and healing within myself.

Life continues to remind us that relationships are more complicated than mainstream media makes them out to be. Where is the movie that shows us what a healthy relationship looks like, in all its beautiful messiness? Who teaches us how to be a partner rather than a servant or mother in our romantic relationships? Where do we learn to fight fair? Why do we stay when we are underappreciated? What about the feeling of home in someone's eyes—what does it mean? Does it mean anything at all? These are questions I continue to grapple with.

I don't believe we are ever explicitly taught how to fully express our emotions and deepest human needs to each other. It is this that becomes tangled and misconstrued in young relationships. The inability to completely and precisely express myself led to the end of the relationships I write of here. And it was these very relationships that have taught me more about myself and the human condition than I believe I would have come to understand otherwise.

I am glad to have learned to recognize my own faults and toxicity. I am grateful to have learned what it feels like to have a boundary crossed. I have shown myself resilience and trustworthiness time and time again. You can, too.

Life is hard. Love is hard. People are messy. None of that means we are not worthy of joy, love, and purpose. It also doesn't mean that we have to lower our standards or live in guilt about the shoulds and ifs we tease ourselves with.

My truest wish for you, reader, is this:

May you know deep within your being that you can never show up late to your own life.

AUTHOR'S NOTE

This is my first book of poetry. I would like to acknowledge that I am a ripe 22 years young, yet I feel certain that because of my experiences, I have wisdom to share with anyone dealing with heartbreak of their own.

This book has been a work of progress over the last three years. This work is my grief-child, the way I have processed and coped with deep feelings for multiple people at the same time. Writing is how I mull over my experiences. What started as scribbles in a journal became an entire record of my emotional journey through both relationships. There will always be old loves and new loves, and their relationships with me will ebb and flow in time. Now, nearly a year after I last spoke with either of my loves, I can say the heartbreak did not make me hostile or bitter. It only made me better at understanding myself and the people I love on this earth. The whole time, I was really just journeying back to myself. Thank you, reader, for walking this path with me.

If these poems meant something to you, please consider writing a review or leaving a rating wherever you purchased this book. Your thoughts will help it connect with others who may find themselves in a similar place and who need to feel like they are not alone.

Finally, to follow my artwork, my poetry, and my continuing journey, follow me on Instagram at @k.elizabethcreates or connect with me at www.kaliedebelak.squarespace.com.

Cheerfully,
Kalie
3/23/22

GRATITUDE

First and foremost, I would like to thank my friends and family who have supported my love for writing since the beginning. Thank you for gifting me journals and sketchbooks over the years and for giving me the space and time to use them. More specifically:

I would like to thank Anna Seltz for reading through one of my roughest drafts and encouraging me to keep refining because something good was happening within the pages.

Thank you to Hanna Ferguson for being both an inspiration and a gentle teacher. You have pushed my poems and expanded the depth of the works I share here. Without your suggestions and commentary, this would certainly not be the book it is now.

To Grace Albright, my dearest friend and confidante. Thank you for listening, reading, suggesting, supporting, and questioning the details of my work. Thank you for imparting your wisdom and being my buddy in this crazy life. Turning my experiences into artwork was undoubtedly inspired and shaped by your hand, too.

Thank you to Mom and Dad. Thanks for loving so big and showing me that it's okay to be completely human. Thanks for demonstrating a healthy relationship that inspires me. Thank you for trusting me as I write vulnerable things that challenge your ideas of public and private. Your support is unceasing, and it doesn't go unnoticed.

Lastly, thank you to my publishing team at Spoonbridge Press—the making of a book is not a one-person job, and I couldn't have made any of this happen without your support, efforts, time, and kindness through the entirety of this project.

www.ingramcontent.com/pod-product-compliance
Lightning Source LLC
Chambersburg PA
CBHW060253150626
46553CB00019BA/2241